This Book Belongs To:

Made in the USA
Monee, IL
20 January 2022

89497431R00066